SHARROW VALE
& THE ANTIQUES QUARTER

SHARROW VALE
& THE ANTIQUES QUARTER

DARREN O'BRIEN

The History Press

First published 2019

The History Press
97 St George's Place, Cheltenham
Gloucestershire, GL50 3QB
www.thehistorypress.co.uk

British Library Cataloguing in Publication Data.
A catalogue record for this book is available from the British Library.

ISBN 978 0 7509 8932 9

Typesetting and origination by The History Press
Printed in Europe

INTRODUCTION

The concept of street photography is a difficult one to pin down; the term itself is misleading and often criticised for trivialising a deep and important photographic practice. In essence, street photography captures the stories of everyday life with the streets being just one of many locations. The American photographer Alex Webb explains it well in his 2014 book *Street Photography and the Poetic Image*: 'Street photography suggests a photographer's particular stance or attitude towards the world, a kind of open-ended exploration with an emphasis on discovery, a sense of wandering that's driven by curiosity rather than an initial idea or goal.' (Webb & Cole, 2014, p50)

Although it is often separated from documentary photography, street photography has similar themes and structures. The main difference is that street photography allows for singular images to stand alone out of context, so images can tell one story. Documentary relies heavily on series of images with a strong narrative. Street photography also relates more strongly to the everyday. It can, therefore, take on a certain historic importance, for example, the images of Cartier Bresson are an important record of Paris in the 1930s.

I have been a street photographer for over eight years and a photographer for much longer. My entry into the subject came while studying Environmental Science at university and, like many, it was the work of the *National Geographic* photographers that inspired me to pick up a camera. During my studies I discovered *Curse of the Black Gold* by Ed Kashi, which made me appreciate the power of the lens to tell a story and form narratives to drive attention to important environmental and social issues.

Street photography initially came to me as a way of documenting the places I visited on my travels and to interact with my environment and meet people even if I could not speak the language. It became an excuse to get out into the world and walk.

This book offered an excellent opportunity to get out and explore my home city of Sheffield, and made me look at my familiar surroundings with more interest. Despite being the fourth largest city in the UK (in terms of population), the main city feels quite small and compact. There is a certain intimacy to Sheffield city centre despite the suburbs spreading for miles over the surrounding hills. When I was asked to suggest an area of focus for the book, it came down to two places: Kelham Island or, the eventual choice, the Antiques Quarter and Sharrowvale.

What sets the Antiques Quarter and Sharrowvale apart is their longstanding history of industry and antiquities, and, more recently, it has become a hub for independent businesses. The area has always been a hive of activity, highlighted by the grand Abbeydale Picture House: built in the 1920s it harks back to an era of prosperity in the area. The cinema and ballroom closed in 1975 and this represented a low period. Over the last twenty years, however, the area has been attracting independent businesses, including shops, cafes and restaurants. It is also famous for the number of antique shops that can be found here, giving the area its name.

The Antiques Quarter included in this book is loosely contained to the spaces between Ecclesial Road and Queens Road. There are roughly five main areas of activity here: Abbeydale Road, London Road, Netheredge, Sharrowvale and Ecclesall Road. Each place has a slightly different vibe, which makes the area interesting. Abbeydale Road and London Road are connected and have a variety of older independent shops and businesses, but have also recently seen a growth of new companies. The area is wonderfully diverse, which holds great interest and appeal. Netheredge is the green area of the city, again with independent shops specialising in organic produce. It has also been in the news recently as the main location of the ongoing protests against the felling of street trees. Sharrowvale sits between Netheredge and the student hub of Ecclesall Road. There is strong a community presence with markets and events held throughout the year. Eccelsall road is a hotbed of student activity and the closest the area has to a high street, with a variety of restaurants and shops, which are, again, mostly independents. It is here that you will find the historic botanical gardens and Endcliffe park. Both parks were opened in the 1880s in a drive to create more green locations in the city. Today they provide beautiful spaces for people to walk, meet and relax in.

I live on the edges of the Antiques Quarter, so it was a great opportunity to explore the area in more detail. I moved here because of the diversity and community that has built up in this part of the city. It also feels like a place going through a period of regeneration, whilst still retaining its core values. The images in this book aim to convey the complex history and diversity of the area, and the developments that will shape its future.

A statue in shadow in the historic Botanical Gardens on Ecclesall Road

Statues for sale in the Antiques Quarter

Moving in different directions. Walking the dogs in the Antiques Quarter

Bragazzis Italian cafe in the Antiques Quarter, coming highly recommended

Relaxing with a coffee and the newspaper at Bragazzis on Abbeydale Road

Opposite: Repurpose and reuse. A selection of chairs on sale on Queens Road, Antiques Quarter

The Botanical Gardens

A nice spot for a picnic in the Botanical Gardens

Waiting for a coffee fix, Ecclesall Road

A busy Bragazzis serving coffee and croissants

Out for a stroll

The corner shop that's hard to miss

Wall art with a powerful message, Abbeydale Road

A cold day to be out and about, Queens Road

A cosy corner for a sit down

Street music at Sharrow Vale market

The hypnotic powers of tie-dye

Fundraising with a mascot at Sharrow Vale market

Monks, Ecclesall Road

Sharrow Vale market

Grabbing a bargain at 'The Pound Zone', a boot fair stall at Abbeydale Picturehouse

Boot fair at Abbeydale Picturehouse

Rummage for a bargain

Browsing the latest offers

Opposite: Modern street art with antique wares

The minarets of The Madina Mosque, Queens Road

Blue skies over Abbeydale Road

A busy corner full of daily goods, Abbeydale Road

Opposite: A unique decoration for the tree, Nether Edge

A sunny display, Abbeydale Road

Window washing, London Road

Plugged in whilst waiting for the bus, London Road

Opposite: Display outside a shop, Nether Edge

A sky with a view, London Road

An innovative veg stall

All the purple, Yama Sushi

Deep in thought, London Road

Sharrow Vale

In conversation

Crossing, London Road

New building works between London Road and Ecclesall Road

London Road shop

Kasem working in his sewing shop on Abbeydale Road

Royal Wedding cut-outs, Ecclesall Road

Yellow, Ecclesall Road

Graffiti, Ecclesall Road

Dog in the sun, Ecclesall Road

Waiting, Ecclesall Road

Cafe window

Lunch on the go

Shopkeeper, Ecclesall Road

Car wash at the bottom of Eccesall Road

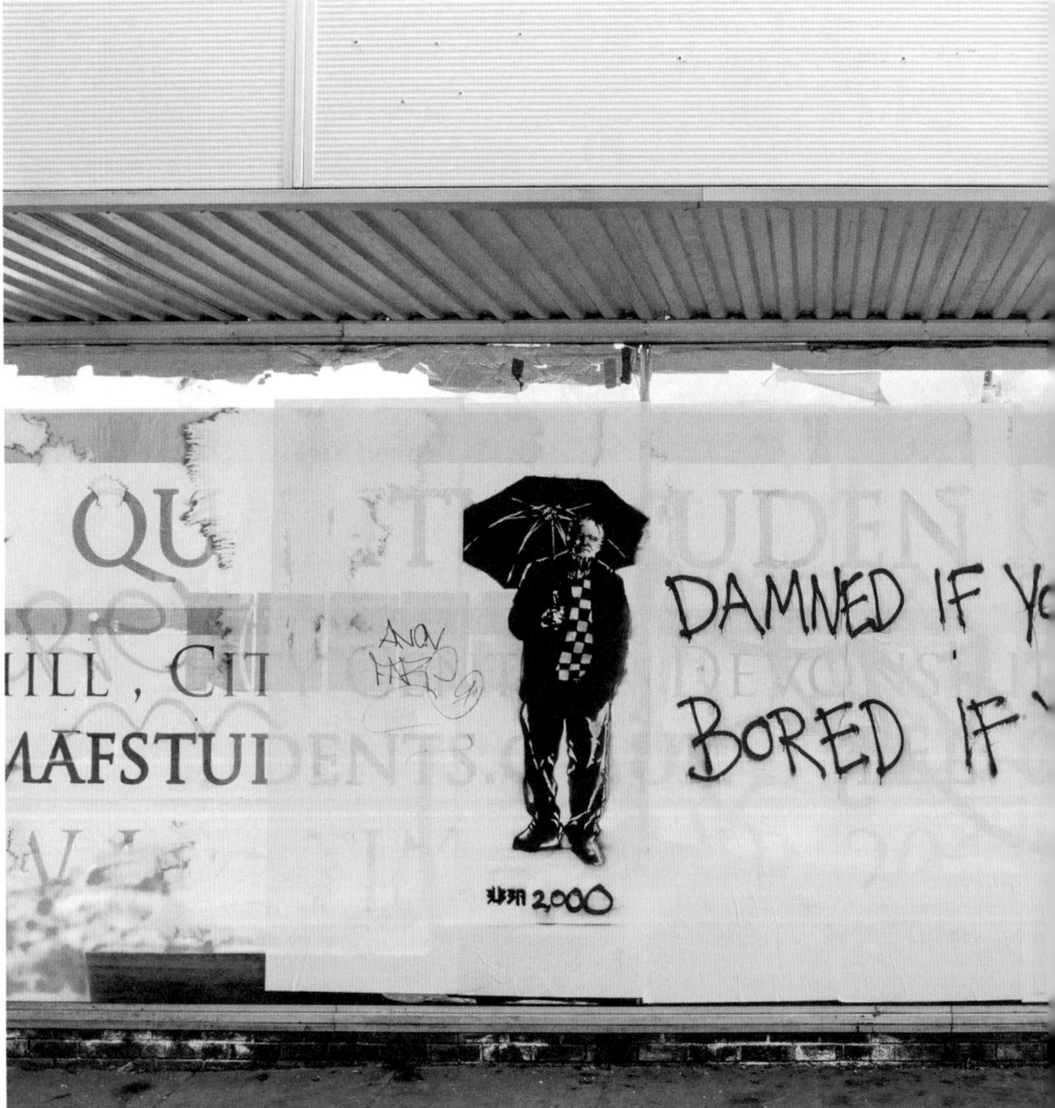
QU
ILL , CIT
MAAFSTUI
DAMNED IF Y
BORED IF
2,000

Inspirational sign

Ice cream, Endcliffe Park

Window seat at The Cremorne pub, London Road

Smoke break, London Road

A busy corner at London Road

Catching up with friends, London Road

The grand structure of the Grade II listed Abbeydale Picture House on Abbeydale Road, the only surviving 1920s cinema in Sheffield

Mother and daughter out walking, Abbeydale Road

One person's junk is another person's treasure

Sweets

Richie outside his mirror shop, Abbeydale Road

Antiques shopping

Dome in the clouds

Drinking en route, Ecclesall Road

The wonderful Cafe No. 9. A great place to catch up with friends

Okay Google, 'Where's the nearest rubbish bin?', Netheredge

Perfect display of Christmas wreaths, Sharrow Vale Christmas market

There's a Father Christmas on every corner in Sharrow Vale Christmas market

A young couple enjoying the Christmas market

Opposite: Waiting for the bus with dog and matching coat, Sharrow Vale

Butchery so good they queue around the corner, with the awning providing convenient shelter

Planting at a Sharrow Vale restaurant

A colourful display giving protection from the rain at the Christmas market

Upcycled benches at the local cafe, Ecclesall Road

Let there be dancing at Cafe No.9

Football at the U-Mix Centre

Barrow Boy Bar, Abbeydale Road

A group drinking outside Barrow Boy Bar

Art in progress, Hagglers Corner

Art in situ, Abbeydale Picture House

Graffiti display surrounding the basketball hoop. Ever inventive and colourful, near London Road

Glen, owner of Okeh Cafe, enjoying a break

Supporters on the way to the match

Enjoying some post-match food

Overleaf: Urban beekeeping at Heeley City Farm, Heeley

Flowers at the city farm, Heeley

Nativity scene outside the Mother of God Catholic church, Abbeydale Road

Browsing the wares, Abbeydale Road

Lots to buy and sell at a busy boot fair at Abbeydale Picture House

Passing the time of day, Abbeydale Road

Browsing the garden planters and chimney pots, Abbeydale Road

Cafe lunch in the sun.

Glen, in one of the booths at Okeh Cafe

Customers seem to enjoy the comfortable seats too

Mulling things over, Bragazzis coffee shop

Catching up over a cuppa at Bragazzis